For Us In Himself:
Contemplations on Our Humanity from the Writings of St. Cyril of Alexandria

For Us In Himself

Contemplations on Our Humanity from the Writings of St. Cyril of Alexandria

Rev. Mark Aziz

AGORA
UNIVERSITY
PRESS

For Us In Himself: Contemplations on Our Humanity from the Writings of St. Cyril of Alexandria

Copyright © 2020 by Agora University Press
Cover art by Kirollos Kilada

All rights reserved. Printed in the United States of America. No part of this book may be used or reproduced in any manner whatsoever without written permission except in the case of brief quotations embodied in critical articles or reviews.
For information contact : aupress@aui.ac
Agora University Press http://www.aui.ac

ISBN 978-1-950831-08-1

HIS HOLINESS POPE TAWADROS II
118th Pope and Patriarch of the great city of Alexandria and the See of St. Mark.

HIS HOLINESS PATRIARCH IGNATIUS APHREM II
Patriarch of Antioch and All the East.

Printed in the United States of America

Acknowledgement

I would like to thank everyone who shared in producing this book, especially Mr. & Mrs. Fischbacher, and Dr. Michael Armanyous who revised the English language. May the Lord bless them all and reward them in the heavenly Jerusalem.

Preface

Our Coptic Orthodox Church, as a faithful mother, always provides us with the pure milk[1] and solid food that belongs to those who are of full age.[2] It is our belief that the Word of God is written by churchmen (Prophets and Apostles), interpreted by Church Fathers, lived and experienced by the Church saints and kept through the centuries by the Church.

In this book we taste one of these Church interpretations and rich experiences through the teachings of St. Cyril the Great, the 24th Pope of Alexandria. I did not add any comments to the quotes, as they are very rich in themselves and basically self-explanatory.

May the True Lamb of God the Father, Who rose from the dead on the third day, guide our steps towards the path of peace, keep us from every evil all the days of our life, and grant us

---

[1] 1 Pet. 2:2
[2] Heb. 5:14

the forgiveness of our sins. Through the never-ending intercessions of the Holy Theotokos Saint Mary, and the prayers of all His angels, apostles, martyrs, saints who have pleased Him since the beginning, and the prayers of His Holiness Pope Tawadros II, we pray that this work would be a source of blessing for the glory of His Name and the spread of His Kingdom. Glory be to the Holy Trinity, our God, unto the ages of all ages, Amen.

Fr. Mark Aziz, M. Th.

Parish Priest of St. Mark Coptic Orthodox Church in Washington, D.C.

The Feast of the Holy Resurrection

22 Baramouda 1731 AM
1 May 2016

v

Abbreviations

ACT *Ancient Christian Texts* (ed. J.C. Elowsky)

ANF *Ante-Nicene Fathers: The Writings of the Fathers Down to A.D. 325* (eds. A.C. Coxe, J. Donaldson, A. Roberts)

LFC *Library of Fathers of the Holy Catholic Church: Anterior to the Division of the East and West* (ed. E.B. Pusey)

NPNF *A Select Library of the Nicene and Post-Nicene Fathers of the Christian Church: Second Series* (ed. P. Scaff)

PG *Patrologica Graeca* (ed. J.P. Migne)

Table of Contents

Acknowledgement	vi
Preface	vii
St. Cyril of Alexandria	11
Introduction	15
Incarnate Offering	20
Receive the Spirit	21
Divine Stability	23
One of Us	25
Newness of Life	27
Confidence with the Father	28
Kenosis	31
The Beginning	33
Access	34
Glory of Adoption	35
Restoration	37
Enthronement	38
Our Mediator	40
Our Advocate	41
Molding Us Anew	42
Union	44
For Us	45
To Conform and To Share	47
The Firstfruits	48

Blending For Union.............................50
Security...52
Conjoined to God............................54
Peace and Goodwill........................55
One with Him..................................57
Re-Bloomed unto Life.....................59
Participation....................................60
Transformation................................62
Spiritual Conformation...................64
Joined and United............................66
The Glory..68
Purveyor and Conqueror.................70
The Power to Conquer....................72
Of Poverty and Riches....................74
Ours for His....................................76
Communion of Grace......................77
Indwelling.......................................79
Ransom on Our Behalf...................81
Return Anew...................................83
Before the Father............................85
A New Root....................................87
His Proper Good.............................89
Partakers...91
To Mold and Renew.......................93
Communion....................................95

Abba, Father	97
Perfects the Imperfect	98
One Entity	99
The Will of the Word	101
Mystical Supper	103
Entwined to Unite	105
Indivisible	107
Eternal Being	109
Gods and Sons	111
The Adoption	113
To Resemble Christ	115
Exalted, Anointed, Sanctified	117
Grace For Grace	119
Transfiguration	121
Breath of Life	123
Ascension	125
To Life	127
To Overcome	128
To Live	129
Trampled Death by Death	130
To Bless	132
To Make Holy	134
Seed of Immortality	136
To Restore	137

St. Cyril of Alexandria

St. Cyril was born around year 378 AD in the small town of Theodosius in Egypt. His mother's brother, St Theophilus, was a priest who was later chosen to be the 23rd Pope of Alexandria. His mother remained close to her brother and under his guidance, St. Cyril was well educated. His education showed through his knowledge, in his writings, of Christian writers of his days, including Eusebius, Origen, Didymus, and several fathers of the Alexandrian church. He showed knowledge of Latin through his extensive correspondence with the Bishop of Rome, Pope Celestine. As for his formal education, he completed grammatical studies at between the age of 12 to 14 years, he studied Rhetoric/Humanities at age 15 to 20 years, and later Christian theology and Biblical studies. He was ordained a Reader by his uncle, Pope Theophilus, in the Church of Alexandria and under his uncle's guidance he advanced in knowledge and church ranks.

Theophilus died on the 15th October 412 AD, and Cyril was made Pope on the 18th October 412 AD, against stiff opposition by the party of the incumbent Archdeacon Timothy in a then volatile atmosphere in Alexandria. Thus, St. Cyril followed first St Athanasius and then Theophilus as the Pope of Alexandria in a position that had become powerful and influential, rivalling that of the city Prefect.

His early years as patriarch were caught up in the problems of a cosmopolitan city where the animosities among the various Christian factions, primarily Jews and pagans, had often led to frequent violence. In addition, at the time there was the well-known rivalry between Alexandria and Constantinople and a clash between Alexandrian and Antiochian schools of ecclesiastical reflection, piety, and discourse. These issues came to a head in 428 AD when the see of Constantinople became vacant. Nestorius, from the Antiochian party, was made Archbishop of Constantinople on the 10th of April 428 AD, and kindled the fires by denouncing the use of the term Theotokos as not a proper rendition of Mary's position in relation to Christ.

Thus, St. Cyril and the Alexandrian party crossed swords with those of the Antiochian party in the imperial home court. After much infighting, Augusta Pulcheria, older sister of the Emperor Theodosius II, sided with St. Cyril against Nestorius. To rid himself of St. Cyril, Nestorius recommended to the emperor a council in Constantinople. However, when Theodosius called the council it was in Ephesus, an area friendly to Cyril. After months of maneuvering, the Council of 431 AD ended with Nestorius being removed from office and sent into exile.

St. Cyril the 24th Pope of Alexandria died on the 10th July 444 AD.[3]

---

[3] Dr. Noshy Abd El-Shaheed, *Lectures in Patristics* (course), second year, second term, 2002, 3-6.

Introduction

St. Cyril of Alexandria is certainly most acknowledged for his understanding of the Incarnation, an understanding that was formulated at the time of the Christological controversy of the Nestorian heresy. His understanding, as voiced in his Second Letter to Nestorius, was accepted by the council of Ephesus (431 AD) as a true expression of Orthodox belief.

As most of the Alexandrian Fathers, he was keen to defend the true doctrine. While he was doing this, he believed that he was defending our own personal salvation. St. Cyril's Christological thought principally and consistently emerged from his soteriological concerns:

> "It was therefore necessary that the Only- Begotten Word of God who brought himself down to the level of self-emptying, should not repudiate the low estate arising

from that self-emptying, but should accept that is full by nature on account of the humanity, not for his own sake, but for ours, who lack every good thing."[4]

Resonating with his predecessors St. Irenaeus[5] and St. Athanasius[6] that the Son of God must become the Son of Man so that the son of man might become the son of God:

> "It is not otherwise possible for man, being of a nature which

---

[4] Isa. 11: 1-3. See also Norman Russell, *Cyril of Alexandria*, The Early Church Fathers (Abington: Routledge 2002), 83.

[5] Irenaeus states the Word of God " became what we are that He might make us what He Himself is." See Alexander Roberts, ANF Vol. 1, (Peabody: Hendrickson, 2012), 354.

[6] St. Athanasius states " He assumed humanity that we might become God" (De Incarn. 54.3). See St. Athanasius, *On The Incarnation*, (Crestwood: St. Vladimir's Press, 2000), 93.

perishes, to escape death, unless he recovered that ancient grace, and partook once more of God who holds all things together in being and preserves the in life through the Son in the Spirit. Therefore his Only-Begotten Word has become a partaker of flesh and blood (Heb 2:14), that is, he has become man, though being Life by Nature, and begotten of the life that is by nature, that is , of God the Father, so that, having untied Himself with the flesh which perishes according to the law of its own nature...He might restore it for his own Life and render it through Himself a partaker of God the Father ... and ours, he wears our nature, refashioning it to His own Life. And He Himself is also in us, for we have all become partakers of Him, and have Him in ourselves through the Spirit. For this reason we have become 'Partakers of the divine nature' (2

Pet 1:4), and are reckoned as sons, and so too we have in ourselves the Father Himself through the Son."[7]

In this book we choose some excerpts from the works of St. Cyril in which he uses one of his famous terms "For us in Himself." This term shows clearly that he was defending our own salvation in his refutation of the Nestorian heresy. It also negates the notion that it was merely an intellectual or theological debate for the cause of debate.

This also confirms the mind of the Nicene creed in which we state: "Who for us and for Our salvation became man." This affirms all that Our Lord Jesus Christ has done was for our sake in Himself.

---

[7] John 14:20. See also *The Theology of St Cyril of Alexandria: A Critical Appreciation*, Thomas G. Weinandy and Daniel Keating, eds. (London: T & T Clark, 2003).

Let us rejoice and enjoy all what He has done for us in Himself in its fullness for the Glory of His Name.

-1-

Incarnate Offer

The Divine Scripture says that Christ has been made the High Priest and Apostle of our Confession and that He offered Himself for us for an odor of a sweet smell to God the Father. If anyone therefore denies that, the Very Word out of God was made our High Priest and Apostle when He was made Flesh and man as we, and says rather that man of a woman apart from himself as other than He, was [so made]: or if any one says that on His own behalf also He offered the Sacrifice and not rather for us alone (for He needed not offering Who knew not sin), be he anathema.[8]

---

[8] Cyril of Alexandria, *Five Tomes against Nestorius*; *Scholia on the Incarnation*; *Christ Is One*; *Fragments against Diodore of Tarsus, Theodore of Mopsuestia, the Synousiasts*, LFC 47 (London: Oxford Press 1881), xii.

-2-

Receive the Spirit

Besides what has been said, we must consider this too. For we shall see by going through wise reasonings, and confirmed thereto by words out of the Divine Scripture, that not for Himself did Christ receive the Spirit, but rather for us in Himself, for all good things flow through Him into us too. For since our forefather Adam, being turned aside by deceit into disobedience and sin, did not preserve the grace of the Spirit, and thus in him the whole nature lost at last the God-given good, God the Word, Who knows no turning, needed to become Man, in order that by receiving as Man, He might preserve the Good permanently to our nature.[9]

---

[9] Cyril of Alexandria, *Commentary on the Gospel according to St. John*, LFC 43 (London: Oxford Press, 1874), 548-549.

-3-

Divine Stability

The Only-Begotten was made, therefore, Man as we, that in Him first the good things returning and the grace of the Spirit rooted might be preserved securely[10] to our whole nature, the Only-Begotten and Word of God the Father lending us the stability[11] of His own nature, because the nature of man had been condemned in Adam as powerless for stability and falling (and that most easily) into perversion. As then in the turning[12] of the first, the loss of good things passes through unto the whole nature: in the same way I deem in Him too, Who knew not turning, will the gain of the

---

[10] ἀραρότως
[11] τὸ ἀμετάπτωτον
[12] τροπαῖς

abidance of the Divine Gifts be preserved to our whole race.[13]

---

[13] Cyril of Alexandria, *Commentary on the Gospel according to St. John*, LFC 43 (London: Oxford Press, 1874), 548-549.

-4-

One of Us

And if we seem to any not to think and speak altogether what is proper,[14] let him come forward and tell us why the Savior has been called by the Divine Scriptures the Second Adam.[15] For in that first one, the human race proceeds from not being unto being, and having come forth, decayed, because it had broken the Divine Law: in the Second Adam, Christ, it rose up again unto a second beginning, reformed unto newness of life and unto a return of incorruption (2 Cor. 5:17), for it ought be in Christ, a new creature, as Paul says. There has therefore been given to us the renewing Spirit, that is, the Holy Spirit, the occasionof everlasting life, after that, Christ was glorified, i.e., after the Resurrection, when having burst the bonds

---

[14] τὰ εἰκότα
[15] 1 Cor. 15:45

of death and appeared superior to all corruption, He lived again having our whole nature in Himself, in that He was Man and One of us.[16]

---

[16] Cyril of Alexandria, *Commentary on the Gospel according to St. John*, LFC 43 (London: Oxford Press, 1874), 548-549.

-5-

Newness of Life

For in the time of his love for us, that is, when he became man for us, He refashioned in Himself the whole of nature unto newness of life,[17] restoring it, as God, to what it had been originally, and thus showed us a supernatural spring, but he also rendered spiritual, through piety, those who were unspiritual because of the sin which had held dominion over them from of old.[18]

---

[17] Cf. Rom. 6:4
[18] Cyril of Alexandria, *Five Tomes against Nestorius*; *Scholia on the Incarnation*; *Christ Is One*; *Fragments against Diodore of Tarsus, Theodore of Mopsuestia, the Synousiasts*, LFC 47 (London: Oxford Press 1881), 297-298.

-6-

Confidence with the Father[19]

Who offered Himself on our behalf for an odor of a sweet smell to God the Father. And hereto will be our warrant: Paul, most learned in the law, has written, "Be therefore imitators of God as beloved children, and walk in love as Christ too loved us and delivered Himself for us an offering and sacrifice to God for an odor of a sweet smell."[20] But since Christ has been made a sweet smell for us showing in Himself the nature of man in possession of sinlessness, we have confidence[21] through Him and in Him with God the Father Who is in heaven: for it is written, Having therefore, brethren, boldness to enter into the holy of holies, in the blood of Christ, which He inaugurated for us, a new and

---

[19] Or boldness.
[20] Eph. 5:1, 2
[21] boldness

living way through the veil, that is, through His flesh.[22] Understand therefore how He says that His is the Blood and His the flesh, which he also calls the veil and with good reason, in order that whatever in the temple the sacred veil used to effect, concealing full well the holy of holies, somewhat of the same might the flesh too of the Lord be conceived of as doing, not permitting the marvelous and choice. Excellence and glory of God the Word to it united, to be seen by any bare, so to say and unhidden. And indeed some imagined that Christ was Elias or one of the prophets,[23] but the Jews, not understanding the mystery respecting Him, railing said, Is this not the carpenter's son?[24] how says He now, I have come down from heaven?[25] For invisible by Nature is the Godhead, yet was He seen of

---

[22] Heb. 10:19, 20

[23] Matt. 16:14

[24] Matt. 13:55. The Syriac translation renders: Jesus, the carpenter's son.

[25] John 6:42

those on earth in likeness with us Who in His own nature is not visible, but the Lord God appeared to us. And this I think the Divine David teaches saying, God shall come manifestly, our God, and shall be passed over in silence.[26]

---

[26] Ps. 50:3. LXX. See also: Cyril of Alexandria, *Five Tomes against Nestorius*; *Scholia on the Incarnation*; *Christ Is One*; *Fragments against Diodore of Tarsus, Theodore of Mopsuestia, the Synousiasts*, LFC 47 (London: Oxford Press 1881), 297-298.

-7-

Kenosis

Therefore through Himself He receives the Spirit for us, and renews to our nature, the ancient good. For thus He also said for our sakes He became poor.[27] For being rich, as God and lacking no good thing, He became man lacking all things.[28] to whom it is somewhere said and that very well, What do you have that you did not receive? As then, being by Nature Life, He died in the flesh for our sakes, that He might overcome death for us, and raise up our whole nature together with Himself (for we were all in Him, in that He was made Man): so does He also receive the Spirit for our

---

[27] 2 Cor. 8:9
[28] 1 Cor. 4:7

sakes, that He may sanctify our whole Nature.[29]

---

[29] Cyril of Alexandria, *Commentary on the Gospel according to St. John*, LFC 43 (London: Oxford Press, 1874), 142-143.

-8-

The Beginning

When the Word of God became Man, He received the Spirit from the Father as one of us, not receiving ought for Himself individually, for He was the Giver of the Spirit, but that He might, by receiving It as Man, preserve It to our nature, and might again root in us the grace which had left us.

For He came not to profit Himself, but to be to all of us, the Door and Beginning and Way of the Heavenly Goods. For if He had not been pleased to receive, as Man, or to suffer too, as one of us, how could anyone have shown that He humbled Himself?[30]

---

[30] On John 1:32 in Cyril of Alexandria, *Commentary on John,* ACT 1 (Downers Grove: InterVarsity Press, 2013), 142-143.

-9-

Access

For heaven was then utterly inaccessible to mortal man, and no flesh as yet had ever trodden that pure and all-holy realm of the angels; but Christ was the first Who consecrated for us the means of access to Himself, and granted to flesh a way of entrance into heaven; presenting Himself as an offering to God the Father, as it were the first fruits of them that are asleep[31] and are lying in the tomb, and the first of mankind that ever appeared in heaven.[32]

---

[31] 1 Cor. 15:20
[32] Cyril of Alexandria, *Commentary on the Gospel according to S. John,* LFC 48 (London: Oxford Press, 1885), 235-238.

-10-

The Glory of Adoption

Therefore our Lord Jesus the Christ consecrated for us a new and living way,[33] as St. Paul says; not having entered into a holy place made with hands,[34] appear before the face of God for us. For it is not that He may present Himself before the presence of God the Father that Christ has ascended up on high: for He ever was and is and will be continually in the Father, in the sight of Him Who begat Him,[35] for He it is in Whom the Father ever takes delight: but now He Who of old was the Word with no part or lot in human nature, has ascended in human form that He may appear in heaven in a strange and unaccustomed manner. And this He has done on our account and for our sakes, in

---

[33] Heb. 10:19
[34] Heb. 9:24
[35] Cf. Prov. 8:23

order that He, though found as a man,[36] may still in His absolute power as Son, while yet in human form, obey the command: Sit at on My right hand,[37] and so may transfer the glory of adoption through Himself to all the race.[38]

---

[36] Phil. 2:8

[37] Ps. 110:1

[38] Cyril of Alexandria, *Commentary on the Gospel according to S. John*, LFC 48 (London: Oxford Press, 1885), 235-238.

-11-

Restoration

He has presented Himself therefore as Man to the Father on our behalf, so that He may restore us, who had been removed from the Father's presence by the ancient transgression, again, as it were, to behold the Father's face. He sits there in His position as Son, so that we also, through Him, may be called sons and children of God. For this reason also Paul, who insists that he has Christ speaking by his voice, teaches us to regard the events that happened in the life of Christ alone as common to the whole race; saying that God raised us up with Him, and made us to sit with Him in the heavenly places, in Christ.[39] -

---

[39] Cyril of Alexandria, *Commentary on the Gospel according to S. John,* LFC 48 (London: Oxford Press, 1885), 235-238. See also Eph. 2:6.

-12-

Enthronement

For to Christ, as by nature Son, it belongs as a special prerogative to sit at the Father's side, and the glory of this dignity we can ascribe rightly and truly to Him, and Him alone. But the fact that Christ Who sits there is in all points like unto us, in that He has appeared as Man, while we believe Him to be God of God, seems to confer on us also the privilege of this dignity. For even if we shall not sit at the side of the Father Himself,—for how could the servant ever ascend to equal honor with the master?—yet nevertheless Christ promised the holy disciples that they should sit on thrones. For He says: When the Son of Man shall sit on the throne of His glory, you also shall sit upon twelve thrones, judging the twelve tribes of Israel.[40]

---

[40] Cyril of Alexandria, *Commentary on the Gospel according to S. John,* LFC 48 (London: Oxford Press, 1885), 235-238. See also Matt. 19:26.

-13-

Our Mediator

He once more mediates as Man, the Reconciler and Mediator of God and men; and being our truly great and all-holy High Priest, by His own prayers He appeases the anger of His Father, sacrificing Himself for us. For He is the Sacrifice, and is Himself our Priest, Himself our Mediator, Himself a blameless Victim, the true Lamb Which took away the sin of the world. The Mosaic ceremonial was then, as it were, a type, and transparent foreshadowing, of the mediation of Christ, shown forth in the last times, and the high priest of the Law indicated in his own person that Priest Who is above the Law.[41]

---

[41] Cyril of Alexandria, *Commentary on the Gospel according to S. John,* LFC 48 (London: Oxford Press, 1885), 235-238.

-14-

Our Advocate

Paul showed us this most plainly in the words: Grace to you and peace from God our Father, and the Lord Jesus Christ.[42] He then prays for us as Man, and also unites in distributing good gifts to us as God. For He, being a holy High Priest, blameless and undefiled, offered Himself not for His own weakness, as was the custom of those to whom was allotted the duty of sacrificing according to the Law, but rather for the salvation of our souls, and that once for all, because of our sin, and is an Advocate for us: and He is the propitiation for our sins, as John says; and not for ours only, but also for the whole world.[43] (John 2:2).

---

[42] 2 Cor. 1:2

[43] John 2:2. See also Cyril of Alexandria, *Commentary on the Gospel according to S. John,* LFC 48 (London: Oxford Press, 1885), 506-507.

-15-

Molding Us Anew

But now are we both partakers and sharers in the Substance that transcends the universe, and are become temples of God. For the Only-Begotten sanctified Himself for our sins; that is, offered Himself up, and brought Himself as a holy Sacrifice for a sweet-smelling aroma to God the Father; that, while He as God came between and hedged off and built a wall of partition between human nature and sin, nothing might hinder our being able to have access to God, and have close fellowship with Him, through communion, that is, with the Holy Spirit, molding us anew to righteousness and sanctification and the original likeness of man.[44]

---

[44] Cyril of Alexandria, *Commentary on the Gospel according to S. John,* LFC 48 (London: Oxford Press, 1885), 537-539.

-16-

Union

For if sin sunders and dissevers man from God, surely righteousness will be a bond of union, and will somehow set us by the side of God Himself, with nothing to part us. We have been justified through faith in Christ, Who was delivered up for our trespasses[45] according to the Scripture, and was raised for our justification. For in Him, as in the first- fruits of the race, the nature of man was wholly reformed into newness of life, and ascending, as it were, to its own first beginning, was molded anew into sanctification.[46]

---

[45] Rom. 4:25
[46] Cyril of Alexandria, *Commentary on the Gospel according to S. John,* LFC 48 (London: Oxford Press, 1885), 537-539.

-17-

For Us

But we must consider that we are here looking upon Him that is beloved from everlasting, as commencing to be loved when He became Man. What, therefore, He then, as it were, took and received, we shall find that He took not for Himself, but for us. For just as, when He lived again after subduing the power of death, He accomplished not His Resurrection for Himself, for He is the Word and God, but gave us this blessing through Himself, and in Himself (for man's nature was in Christ in its entirety, fast bound by the chains of death); in like manner we must suppose that He received the Father's love, not for Himself, because He was continually beloved of Him from the beginning, but rather He accepts it at His Hand upon His

Incarnation, that He may call down upon the Father's love.[47]

---

[47] Cyril of Alexandria, *Commentary on the Gospel according to S. John,* LFC 48 (London: Oxford Press, 1885), 555-556.

-18-

To Conform and To Share

Just as, then, we shall be, nay, we are even now, as in Christ first the Firstfruits of our race, made conformable to His Resurrection and His glory, even so are we, as it were, like Him; beloved, but yielding the supremacy in all things to the Only-begotten, and justly marveling at the incomparable mercy of God, shown towards us; Who showers, as it were, upon us the things that are His, and shares with His creatures what appertains to Himself alone.[48]

---

[48] Cyril of Alexandria, *Commentary on the Gospel according to S. John,* LFC 48 (London: Oxford Press, 1885), 555-556.

-19-

The Firstfruits

For what can be raised up save that which is fallen? or what restored to life, save that which is bowed down in death? And how shall we expect to rise again, if so that Christ raised not up His own Temple, making Himself, for us, the Firstfruits of them which are asleep, and the Firstborn from the dead? Or how shall this mortal put on immortality,[49] if, as some think, it be lost in total annihilation? For how shall it escape this fate if it have no hope of a new life? Do not, then, swerve from orthodoxy in the faith, because a miracle was accomplished; but rather be wise, and add

---

[49] 1Cor 15:53.

this to the other marvelous works that Christ did.[50]

---

[50] Cyril of Alexandria, *Commentary on the Gospel according to S. John,* LFC 48 (London: Oxford Press, 1885), 666-667.

-20-

Blending for Union

The Only-begotten, then, proceeding from the very Substance of God the Father, and having entirely in His own nature Him That begat Him, became Flesh according to the Scripture, bending Himself, as it were, with our nature by an unspeakable combination and union with this body that is earthly; and thus He that is God by nature became, and is in truth, a Man from heaven... in order that, uniting as it were in Himself things widely opposed by nature, and adverse to fusion with each other, He might enable man to share and partake of the nature of God.

For even unto us has reached the fellowship and abiding Presence of the Spirit, which originated through Christ and in Christ first, when He is in fact become even as we are, that is, a Man, receiving unction and sanctification, though He is by nature God [...] the Mystery, then, that is in Christ is become, as it were, a beginning and a way whereby we may partake of the Holy Spirit and union with God.[51]

---

[51] On John 17 in in Cyril of Alexandria, *Commentary on John,* ACT 1 (Downers Grove: InterVarsity Press, 2013), 251.

-21-

Security

We must inquire what sense it may be seemly to conceive that God the Father condemned sin in the flesh by sending His own Son in likeness of sinful flesh.[52] For albeit the Son was by nature God and had shone forth from His essence and possessed naturally the immutability of His proper being, and for this cause in no wise could stumble into sin, or turn aside into what is not right, the Father caused Him voluntarily to descend into the flesh that is subject to sin, with intent that making very flesh His own, He might bring it over unto His own natural property, that is to say, sinlessness.

For, I conceive, we shall not be right in believing that it was with intent to effect this for the Temple of His own Body alone

---

[52] Rom. 8:3

that the Only-begotten has been made man; for where were the glory and profit of His advent unto us to be seen, if He accomplished the salvation of His own Body alone? But we believe rather that it was to secure the benefits for all nature through Himself and in Himself as in the firstfruits of humanity, that the Only-Begotten became like us.[53]

---

[53] On John 14:20 in Cyril of Alexandria, *Commentary on John,* ACT 1 (Downers Grove: InterVarsity Press, 2013), 316-317.

-22-

Conjoined to God

The mediation of Moses was ministrative, that of Christ is free and more mystical, in that He takes hold by Nature of the things mediated and reaches unto both, I mean the manhood that is mediated and God the Father.

For He was by Nature God, as the Only-Begotten of God, as not separated from the Essence of Him Who begat Him, and in being in It, as He is conceived to be also of it. But He was Man too, in that He became Flesh likening Himself to us, that through Him that which is by nature far separated might be conjoined to God.[54]

---

[54] On John 5:46 in Cyril of Alexandria, *Commentary on John,* ACT 1 (Downers Grove: InterVarsity Press, 2013), 308-309.

-23-

Peace and Goodwill

How noble was the hymn, "Glory to God in the highest, and on earth peace, and among men good will!"[55] For we, wretched beings, by having set up our own lusts in opposition to the will of our Lord, had put ourselves into the position of enemies unto Him. But by Christ this has been done away: for He is our peace; for He has united us by Himself unto God the Father, having taken away from the middle the cause of the enmity, even sin, and so justifies us by faith, and calls near unto Him those who were afar off: and besides this, He has created the two people into one new man, so making peace and reconciling both in one body to the Father.

For it pleased God the Father to gather into one new whole all things in Him, and to

---

[55] Luke 2:14

bind together things below and things above, and to make those in Heaven and those on earth into one flock. Christ therefore has been made for us both Peace and Goodwill.[56]

---

[56] On Luke 2: 8-18 in B. Payne Smith, *The Commentary on the Gospel of St. Luke by St. Cyril of Alexandria,* Part I, Volume XII (Kent: Oriental Orthodox Library, 2007), 16-17.

-24-

One with Him

The life-giving power of God the Father is the Only-begotten Word: and Him He sent to us as a Savior and Deliverer. He became flesh, not by having undergone any change or alteration into what He had been, nor again by having ceased to be the Word, but rather by having been born in the flesh of a woman, and taken unto Himself that body which He received from her, in order that He might implant Himself in us by an inseparable union […] The Word therefore, by having united unto Himself that flesh which was subject unto death, as being God and Life drove away from it corruption and made it also to be life-giving […] When therefore we eat the holy flesh of Christ, the Savior of us all, and drink His precious blood, we have life in us, being made as it were, one with Him, and abiding in Him, and possessing Him also in us.[57]

---

[57] On Luke 22:19 in B. Payne Smith, *The Commentary on the Gospel of St. Luke by St. Cyril of Alexandria,* Part I, Volume XII (Kent: Oriental Orthodox Library, 2007), 666-668.

-25-

Re-Bloomed unto Life

Since the Only-Begotten Word of God being Life by Nature was made flesh, the nature of man rebloomed unto life: for He has become first in everything.[58] And for this reason the Life-giving Word of God made the flesh which was subject to death, His own, in order that manifesting it superior to both death and decay, He might transmit the grace to us too. For as in Adam we were brought down unto death, so in Christ thrusting aside the tyranny of death, are we reformed unto immortality.[59]

---

[58] Col 1:18
[59] Cyril of Alexandria, *Against Diodore of Tarsus and Theodore of Mopsuestia* (Fragments of the Second Book), LFC 47 (London: Oxford Press, 1881), 338.

-26-

Participation

I should like to learn what was the purpose of His coming among us; what was the mode of His incarnation, and the reason for it.

Is it not quite obvious and unambiguous to everyone, that the Only begotten became like us, that is a complete man, that He might free our earthly body from the corruption which had been brought into it?

By becoming the Flesh of the Word, who gives life to all things, this Flesh triumphs over the power of death and destruction. In the same way, no doubt, the soul, since it has become the soul of Him who had no experience of doing wrong, has its state secured, immutable in all good, and incomparably stronger than the sin which before exercised domination. For Christ is the first man who committed no sin and was convicted of no dishonesty. He is, so to speak, the root and the first fruits of those who are restored in the Spirit to newness of life, to immortality of the body, to certainty and security of divinity, so that He may transmit this condition to the whole of humanity by participation, and as an act of grace.[60]

---

[60] Cyril of Alexandria, *Dialogue on the Incarnation of the Only-Begotten,* (PG 75: 1213).

-27-

Transformation

"My Son are You, This day have I begotten You."[61] Him Who was God before ages and was begotten of Him, (the Father) says that He has this day begotten, that in Him He may receive us into sonship, for the whole human nature was in Christ, in that He was Man. So is the Father said to give the Spirit again to the Son Who has It as His own Spirit, that we in Him may gain the Spirit.

The Only-Begotten therefore receives the Holy Ghost not for Himself [...] but having been made Man, He had our whole nature in Himself, that He might uplift it all transforming it unto its first state. We see then that not for Himself did Christ receive the Spirit, but rather for us in Himself, for

---

[61] Ps 2: 7

all good things flow through Him into us too.[62]

---

[62] On John 7:39 Cyril of Alexandria, *Commentary on John,* ACT 1 (Downers Grove: InterVarsity Press, 2013), 548.

-28-

Spiritual Conformation

The Son came, as I said, and was made man, transelementing our estate as in Himself first unto a holy and admirable and truly marvelous birth and life: and Himself first became born of the Holy Spirit, I mean as to the flesh, in order that, the grace passing through Him as by a path unto ourselves too, we having not from blood nor from the will of the flesh nor from the will of man but from God[63] through the Spirit our souls' new birth and spiritual conformation unto the Son who is by nature and truly, might thus abide undecaying, as possessing no longer the first father, Adam, in whom we decayed. And verily Christ said, at one time, And call no

---

[63] John 1:13

one your father on earth, for one is your Father which is in Heaven.[64]

---

[64] Matt 23:9. See also Cyril of Alexandria, *Christ is One,* LFC 47 (London: Oxford Press 1881), 250.

-29-

Joined and United

God the Word came down to the emptiness[65] without being compelled to, but according to His own will and the pleasure of His Father, He became man. While completely preserving the attributes of His own nature without decrease or change, He assumed the human nature according to the divine plan. He is considered One Son of twain, of both natures: the Divine and the human, as they were joined and united together in His one being in an indescribable and inexplicable manner to form one unit in an unimaginable way [...] for He is God and at the same time man.

For that reason He is also considered a Mediator (between God and men), because the two who were, according to nature,

---

[65] cf. Phil 2:7

very much apart from each other, as an immeasurable chasm separated them, that is, the divine and the human, He revealed joined and united in Himself, thus binding us through Himself to God, His Father.[66]

---

[66] Cyril of Alexandria, *Dialogue 1 On The Trinity* (PG 75:659-712).

-30-

The Glory

For the voice of God the Father spoke unto Christ at the time of holy baptism, as though having by Him and in Him accepted man upon earth to the sonship: "This is my beloved Son."[67] For He Who is the Son by nature and in truth, and the Only-begotten, when He became like unto us, is specially declared to be the Son of God, not as receiving this for Himself, for He was and is, as I said, very God – but that He might ratify the glory unto us. For He has been made our first fruits, and firstborn, and second Adam: for which reason it is said, that in Him all things have become new.[68] For having put off the oldness that was in

---

[67] Mat 3:17
[68] 2 Cor 5:17

Adam, we have gained the newness that is in Christ.[69]

---

[69] On Luke 3: 21-23 in B. Payne Smith, *The Commentary on the Gospel of St. Luke by St. Cyril of Alexandria,* Part I, Volume XII (Kent: Oriental Orthodox Library, 2007), 47-48.

-31-

Purveyor and Conqueror

Christ appeared superior to, and stronger than, every sin and worldly hindrance; and since He has conquered, He will also bestow the power to conquer upon such as are tempted for His sake [...] the power of His acts will surely extend even unto us, since He who conquered was one of us, insomuch as He was Incarnate Man. And as we overcome sin that wholly died in Christ first, Christ, that is, being the purveyor to us of the blessing as His own kindred; so also we ought to be of good cheer, because we shall overcome the world; for Christ as Man overcame it for our sakes, being herein the Beginning and the Gate and the Way for the race of man. For we who once were fallen and vanquished have now overcome and are conquerors, through Him Who conquered as one of ourselves, and for our sakes. For if He conquered as God, then it profits us nothing; but if as Man, we are in Him conquerors.[70]

---

[70] On John 16:33; See *The Catechetical Lectures of St Cyril of Alexandria*, LFC 2 (London: Oxford Press 1845), 476-477.

-32-

The Power to Conquer

He took the form of a slave and was made in the likeness of men: for so did He as one of us set Himself as an avenger in our stead, against that murderous and rebellious serpent, who had brought sin upon us [...], that we by His means, and in Him, might gain the victory, whereas of old we were vanquished, and fallen in Adam.

Observe then how the nature of man in Christ casts off the faults of Adam's gluttony: by eating we were conquered in Adam, by abstinence we conquered in Christ.

We therefore won the victory in Christ: and he who conquered in Adam went away ashamed, that we might have him under our feet; for Christ as Conqueror handed on to us also the power to conquer, saying,

"Behold I have granted you to tread upon serpents, and scorpions, and all the power of the enemy."[71]

---

[71] Luke 10:19. See also On Luke 4:1-14 in B. Payne Smith, *The Commentary on the Gospel of St. Luke by St. Cyril of Alexandria,* Part I, Volume XII (Kent: Oriental Orthodox Library, 2007), 49, 54- 56.

-33-

Of Poverty and Riches

He Who by nature is a Son took the form of a slave, [not that by taking upon Him our state, He might continue in the measure of slavery], but that He might set us free, we who were chained to the yoke of slavery, enriching us with what is His.

For through Him and with Him we have received the name of sons. He Who was rich shared our poverty, that He might raise man's nature to His riches [...] we have seen Satan fall, that haughty one laid low, him in contempt and scorn, who once was worshipped: him who seemed a God, put under the feet of the saints: for they received power to rebuke the unclean spirits, and this power is a very great honor, and too high for human nature, and fit only for the supreme God. And of this too the Word manifested in human form was the first to set us the example: for He also rebuked the impure spirits.[72]

---

[72] On Luke 10:23-24 in B. Payne Smith, *The Commentary on the Gospel of St. Luke by St. Cyril of Alexandria,* Part I, Volume XII (Kent: Oriental Orthodox Library, 2007), 308-309.

-34-

Ours for His

When the weak aspects of his emptiness seem to you to be difficult to understand, wonder rather at the great love of the Son for us. For what you say to be improper, this He made voluntarily for your sake. He wept as man that He might stay your tear; He feared, economically committing to His flesh to suffer what belonged it, that He might make us of fairest courage [...] He is said to be weak in His humanity that He might end your weakness. He prolonged prayers and supplications in order that He might render the Father's ear open to your prayers.[73]

---

[73] Cyril of Alexandria, *Letter of Cyril to John, Bishop of Antioch, Against Theodoret*, NPNF II.3 (Grand Rapids: Christian Classics Ethereal Library), 805.

-35-

Communion of Grace

The Word of God has dwelt in us and has made the human flesh his own property. Hence, all that affected this flesh from the cruel law of sin [...] he annulled by himself. For he had mortified it in his own flesh, and has thenceforth emanated within us the communion of this grace. For we are akin to him according to the nature of the flesh.

Since our nature has already renewed its form in Christ, assuming its original holiness, no one should doubt that this grace of renewal is henceforth spreading into the rest of the human race. For the Word was not renewing Himself as God, as being the Uncreated exact representation of the Father, but we it was that were renewed with Him after the likeness of God, with the sanctity which surpasses the nature, the law of sin being put to death in our members.[74]

---

[74] On Matt 11:18

-36-

Indwelling

Just as death was brought to naught in no other way than by the Death of the Savior, so also with regard to each of the sufferings of the flesh: for unless He had felt dread, human nature could not become free from dread; unless He had experienced grief, there could never have been any deliverance from grief; unless He had been troubled and alarmed, no escape from these feelings could have been found. And with regard to every one of the affections to which human nature is liable, you will find exactly the corresponding thing in Christ. The affections of His Flesh were aroused, not that they might have the upper hand as they do indeed in us, but in order that when aroused they might be thoroughly subdued by the power of the Word dwelling in the flesh, the nature of man thus undergoing a change for the better.

For the Word of God made one with Himself human nature in its entirety, that so He might save the entire man. For that which has not been taken [by Him], has not been saved.[75]

---

[75] On John 12:27; See *The Catechetical Lectures of St Cyril of Alexandria,* LFC 2 (London: Oxford Press 1845), 154, 152.

-37-

Ransom for Us

One Lamb died for all, bringing the whole flock on earth back safely to God the Father; one for all, that he might bring all under subjection to God; one for all, that he might gain them all; "that for the future they might all no longer live for themselves, but for him who died and rose again for them."[76] For when we were guilty of many sins, and for that reason were liable to death and destruction, the Father gave his Son a ransom for us, one for all, since all are in him, and he is greater than all. One died for all, that we all might live in him: Death devoured the Lamb on behalf of all, and then vomited all in him, and with him. For we were all in Christ, who died

---

[76] 2 Cor. 5:15

and rose again on our account, and on our behalf.[77]

---

[77] On John 1:29 in *Commentary on the Gospel according to St. John*, LFC 43 (London: Oxford Press, 1874), 132.

-38-

Return Anew

In what manner can man upon earth, clothed as he is with mortality, return to incorruption? I answer, that this dying flesh must be made partaker of the life-giving power which comes from God. But the life-giving power of God the Father is the Only-begotten Word: and Him He sent to us as a Savior and Deliverer. And He became flesh [...] in order that, having implanted Himself in us by an inseparable union, He might raise us above the power both of death and corruption.

For He clothed Himself in our flesh, that by raising it from the dead He might prepare a way henceforth, by which the flesh which had been humbled unto death might return anew unto incorruption [...] and Paul testifies "For as by man is death, by man is also the resurrection of the dead."[78] The Word therefore, by having united unto Himself that flesh which was subject unto death, as being God and Life drove away from it corruption, and made it also to be the source of life. When therefore we eat the holy flesh of Christ, the Savior of us all, and drink His precious blood, we have life in us, being made as it were, one with Him, and abiding in Him, and possessing Him also in us.[79]

---

[78] 1 Cor. 15:21
[79] On Luke, 22:19 in B. Payne Smith, *The Commentary on the Gospel of St. Luke by St. Cyril of Alexandria,* Part I, Volume XII (Kent: Oriental Orthodox Library, 2007), 666-668.

-39-

Before the Father

In what sense does "He now appear in the presence of God on our behalf?" Did he not always appear in God's presence before His incarnation?

It is self-evident that such had been the case, for He is the creative Wisdom of God the Father through Whom all things passed out of nothing into existence, and in which the Father delighted since eternity.[80]

But now He appears in the Father's presence not as the un-incarnate Logos as He had been from the beginning, but in our own form and our own nature. For this reason we say that He appears now "on our behalf" in the presence of God the Father to present our own nature to Him, that

---

[80] Prov. 8:30

nature which had been cast away from His presence on account of Adam's violation.

It is we, therefore, whom He brings before the Father's eyes in His own Person as our beginning Who has become man to bring us closer to the Father.[81]

---

[81] Heb. 9:24. See also, Cyril of Alexandria, *Commentary on the Epistle to the Hebrews* (PG 74:954-1006), trans. HG Bishop Epiphanius.

-40-

A New Root

As sprung from corruptible root, corruptible are we too, and abide (wretched!) held in the meshes of death. But when the Creator planned good things concerning us and willed to transelement the nature of man, decay being taken away, unto what it was at the beginning, He adorned a new root (so to speak) for us, which endured not to be overmastered by death, the One Lord Jesus the Christ, that is God the Word out of His essence made man as we, made of a woman.

Even He be said to suffer, we know that He is Impassible as God, we say that He has suffered death economically in His own flesh, in order that by treading it and rising from it, in that He is Life and Life-giving, He might transelement unto incorruption that which is tyrannized over by death, i.e. the body: and so unto us too spreads the might of the achievement, extending unto the whole race [...] for He lived anew from the dead, having all in Himself.[82]

---

[82] Cyril of Alexandria, *Against Nestorius* (5.1) LFC 47 (London: Oxford Press 1881), 156-157, 159, 161.

-41-

His Proper Good

In no other way was it possible to shake off the cheerless mastery of death save only by only the Incarnation of the Only-Begotten. Therefore has He appeared as we and He made His own a body subject to decay according to the inherent plan of its nature, in order that since Himself is Life (for He has been begotten of the Father Which is Life) He might implant therein His Proper Good, life [...] He has too the name of the last Adam, as made out of Adam according to the flesh and a second beginning of those on earth, the nature of man being transelemented in Him unto newness of life, life in holiness and incorruption through the resurrection from the dead. For thus was death done to nought, in that the Life by nature endured not to submit its own body to decay, because it was not possible that Christ should be held by it[83] according to the voice of the most wise Peter, and thus passed through unto us too the good from this achievement.[84]

---

[83] Acts 2:24
[84] Cyril of Alexandria, *Christ is One*, LFC 47 (London: Oxford Press 1881), 311-312.

-42-

Partakers

Herein does the Word out of God the Father restore us too, rendering us partakers of His own Divine Nature through the Spirit. He has therefore brothers like to Himself and bearing the image of His Divine Nature, in regard of holiness; for thus is Christ formed in us, the Holy Ghost as it were transelementing us from things human unto those that are His own.

Therefore to us too said the blessed Paul, but you are not in the flesh, but in the spirit.[85] Therefore the Son does not transfer anything that has transfers not ought at all of things that have been made into the Nature of His own Godhead (for that were impossible): but there is impressed on those who have been made partakers of His

---

[85] Rom.8:9

Divine Nature through their partaking of the Holy Ghost the spiritual Likeness with Him, and the Beauty of the Ineffable Godhead flashes upon the souls of the saints.[86]

---

[86] Cyril of Alexandria, *Against Nestorius* (3.2) LFC 47 (London: Oxford Press 1881), 94-95.

-43-

To Remold and Renew

Sin has actually been condemned, since it was first mortified in Christ, and would also be mortified in us, once we allow Christ to dwell in our hearts through faith, and through the communion of the Spirit, who renders us conformed to the image of Christ,[87] namely by sanctifying us through virtue. For the Spirit of Christ our Savior is, as it were, His form, and it is He Who somehow impresses upon us by Himself the very Image of God.

However, the Spirit should be considered as Spirit and not as Son; or rather, He is the Spirit of the Son, Who remolds those in whom He dwells through communion, and renews them in the likeness of the Son, so that once God the Father sees in us the features of His own Son which befit Him,

---

[87] Rom 8:29

He loves us also as His children, and dawns upon us with honors that surpass this world.[88]

---

[88] Cyril of Alexandria, *Festal Letters 1-12*, Fathers of the Church Patristic Series 118, ed. J.J. O'Keefe, trans. P.R Amadon, (Washington, D.C.: Catholic University of America Press, 2009), 78.

-44-

Communion

It was impossible for us who had once fallen away through the original transgression to be restored to our pristine glory, except we obtained an ineffable communion and unity with God... But no man can attain to union with God, save by communion with the Holy Spirit, Who implants in us the sanctification of His own Person, and molds anew into His own life the nature which had fallen into corruption, and so brings back to God and to His Likeness that which was bereft of the glory that this confers.

And the Son is the express Image of the Father, and His Spirit is the natural Likeness of the Son. For this cause, molding anew, as it were, into Himself the souls of men, He stamps them with the

Likeness of God, and seals them with the Image of the Most High.[89]

---

[89] On John 17:20-21; See *The Catechetical Lectures of St Cyril of Alexandria,* LFC 2 (London: Oxford Press 1845), 545-546.

-45-

Abba, Father!

St. Paul also writes: "The Spirit Himself bears witness with our spirit that we are children of God."[90] As the Holy Spirit is from the same essence of Him Who gives Him to saints, I mean the same essence of Christ; and as the Word of God dwelling in us through the Spirit and being thus in us, we ascend to the rank of adoption, as having the Son in us, and we are transformed to His form through the fellowship of His Spirit, and thus we rise to His same confidence and have the temerity to cry out: "Abba, Father!" Therefore the Holy Spirit is God because He makes those who receive Him gods.[91]

---

[90] Rom. 8:16
[91] Cyril of Alexandria, *Thesaurus de sancta consubstantiali trinitate* (PG 75:33).

-46-

Perfects the Imperfect

This same sanctifying power that emanates naturally from the Father, offering perfection to the imperfect, is what we name the Holy Spirit. It is superfluous then, as it seems, to imagine something else as an agent with which the Spirit sanctifies creation. For it is not above God's philanthropy to come to the least of beings and sanctify them with the Holy Spirit, as all are His creation [...] therefore the Holy Spirit works in us by Himself, truly sanctifying us and unifying us with Himself due to our clinging to Him, making us partakers of the divine nature.[92]

---

[92] cf. 2 Pet. 1:4. See also Cyril of Alexandria, *Thesaurus de sancta consubstantiali trinitate* (PG 75:34).

-47-

One Entity

For he says: "You shall make the tabernacle with ten curtains of fine twined linen and blue and purple and scarlet stuff... Five curtains shall be coupled to one another; and the other five curtains shall be coupled to one another."[93] The curtains are thus ten, firmly tied to each other. For there are many rooms in the Father's house.[94] The aim of all who live there is certainly one and holy, since the knowledge of God is one and the same, for God has called us to peace as it is written.[95] You will then admit, once it is clear to you, that ten curtains are the fullness of churches in the whole world, as you may suppose, which do not differ in their views nor are odds in their beliefs, but are one in the Spirit. It is

---

[93] Ex. 26:1,3
[94] John 14:2
[95] 1Cor. 7:15

as if they were tied together to form one entity, like that which is in Christ, by faith. For in all churches everywhere the Lord is but one, faith is but one, baptism is but one.[96]

---

[96] Eph. 4:5. See also Cyril of Alexandria, *Worship in Spirit and Truth* (PG 68:133-1126).

-48-

The Will of the Word

How are we supposed to understand the saying which is: "As You and I are one, that even they may be one, I in them and You in Me, that they may become perfectly one?"[97]

As it is the will of the Word of God to bestow upon mankind a most great and supernal grace, He draws each and every one into a union with Himself. Since He has borne a human body He has come to be in us, but on the other hand, He has the Father in Himself, being His Word and His Effulgence. He says, then, "As I am in them, because I have put on the selfsame body as theirs, and as You, Father, are in Me, because I am of Your self-same essence, so I want that they also may be blended with one another, bound together

---

[97] Cf. John 17:22-23

in a sort of unity, and they, having become as one body, should all be in Me, the bearer of them all in the one and only Temple which I have assumed, and so that they may both be and appear as perfected. For I am perfect, even having become a man."[98]

---

[98] Cyril of Alexanria, *Thesaurus de sancta consubstantiali trinitate* (PG 75:12).

-49-

The Mystical Supper

Together let us hasten to the Mystical Supper. Today Christ feeds us, today Christ serves us, Christ, the Lover of Mankind, refreshes us! O awesome mystery! O inexpressible economy! O incomprehensible condescension! O unsearchable kindness! The Creator offers Himself to the creature for his enjoyment! Life itself bestows Himself on mortals for their food and drink! "Come, eat my bread," He urges, "and drink the wine I have mixed for you."[99] "Eat me, Life, and you will live, for this is my desire. Eat the Life that does not fail; for this have I come, that you may have life, and have it more abundantly.[100] Eat the bread which renews your nature. Drink the wine, the exultation of immortality [...] I became like you, for

---

[99] Prov. 9:5
[100] John 10:10

you, without being changed from my nature, that you might through me become partakers of the divine nature."[101]

---

[101] 2 Pet 1:4. See also Thomas Halton, *The Church*, Message of the Fathers of the Church 4 (Wilington: Michael Glazier, 1816), 149-152.

-50-

Entwined to Unite

Just as the root of the vine ministers and distributes to the branches the enjoyment of its own natural and inherent qualities, so the Only- begotten Word of God imparts to the Saints, as it were, an affinity to His own nature which is that of God the Father, by giving them the Spirit... And the Savior Himself says: He that eats My Flesh and drinks My Blood, abides in Me, and I in him. For here it is especially to be observed that Christ says that He shall be in us, not by a certain relation only, as entertained through the affections, but also by a natural participation. For as, if one entwines wax with other wax and melts them by fire there results of both one, so through the participation of the Body of Christ and of

His precious Blood, He in us, and we again in Him, are co-united.[102]

---

[102] On John 15:1; See *The Catechetical Lectures of St Cyril of Alexandria,* LFC 2 (London: Oxford Press 1845), 364, 370.

-51-

Indivisible

Although we are divided by distinctive personalities, I mean, the special personality of each of us, by which each one is either Peter or John, and another Thomas or Matthew, yet we all became of the same body (σύσσωμοι) in Christ, because we are nourished from one flesh, and because we were sealed to be unified through the One Holy Spirit.

As Christ is indivisible, for He is in no way divided, we are all one in Him. Accordingly He said to His Father in heaven: "That they may be one just as We are one."[103] It is clear from this that through being in Christ, and in the Holy Spirit, we

---

[103] John 17:22

are all one according to the body and according to the Spirit.[104]

---

[104] Cyril of Alexandria, *Dialogue 1 On The Trinity* (PG 75:659-712).

Eternal Being

"But when He brought the Firstborn into the world, He said, And let all the angels of God worship Him."[105] For though He is the Only-begotten as regards His divinity, yet as having become our brother, He has also the name of Firstborn; that, being made the first- fruits as it were of the adoption of men, He might make us also the sons of God.[106]

Due to the Father's love to his creatures, the Son named Himself "the Firstborn of all creation,"[107] [...] for He is a First-born for our sake, that the whole creation may be grafted into him as if into a new

---

[105] Heb. 1:6
[106] On Luke 2:7 in B. Payne Smith, *The Commentary on the Gospel of St. Luke by St. Cyril of Alexandria,* Part I, Volume XII (Kent: Oriental Orthodox Library, 2007), 9.
[107] Col. 1:15

immortal origin, and so sprout again out of the eternal Being himself.[108]

---

[108] Cyril of Alexandria, *Thesaurus de sancta consubstantiali trinitate* (PG 75: 25).

-53-

Gods and Sons

(The Word) lowered Himself, in order to lift to His own height that which was lowly by nature; and He bore the form of a slave, though by nature He was Lord and Son, in order to transport what was slave by nature to the glory of adoptive sonship, after His own likeness, with reference to Him. Therefore, just as He became like us, that is, man, in order that we might become like Him, I mean gods and sons, He takes to Himself what is properly ours and gives us in return what is His [...] we mount to the dignity, which is supernatural through our likeness to Him; for we have been called sons of God, even though we are not sons by nature.

By nature and in reality the God of the universe is the Father of Christ; but that does not make Him our Father by nature; rather is He God, as Creator and Lord. But the Son, as it were mingling Himself with us, bestows on our nature the dignity that is properly and peculiarly His own, giving the name of common Father to How own Begetter.[109]

---

[109] On John 20:17; See *The Catechetical Lectures of St Cyril of Alexandria,* LFC 2 (London: Oxford Press 1845), 663-664.

-54-

The Adoption

The word "today" alludes to the time of His coming at which He became flesh remaining as He is, according to nature, Lord of all! For John bore witness to Him saying "He came to His own"[110] alluding through the word "His own" to the world. Then He says as being called to the glory of Kingship "I was set King through Him" i.e., through God the Father. He accepted this matter, so that receiving as man the adoption, although being Son according to nature, He would open up through Himself the way for human nature to share the adoption, calling to the Kingdom of Heaven those under the tyranny of sin. As any inheritance given by a father reaches the whole race emanating from him, so in the same way did we receive the result of Adam's disobedience, and bore the curse

---

[110] John 1:11

and death. In the same manner the blessings of light that are in Christ are extended from Him to the entire human race. The Only-begotten receives then whatever He receives for us, and not at all for Himself, for He is perfect, because He is by nature God.[111]

---

[111] On Psalm 2:7 in Cyril of Alexandria, *On the Psalms* (PG 69:721).

-55-

To Resemble Christ

Due to His great and limitless love for humanity, the Word of God united Himself to us, not to transform Himself to what is ours, as He is unchangeable and immutable, but rather to merge us with Himself, and thus transfer to us that which is His. For receiving Him due to His dwelling in flesh, we consequently have acquired all that is His. We were named sons and also gods, although that is not ours according to nature, as it is His, but according to grace. In the same manner, He also, when He merged with us becoming man, bore our weaknesses and was considered as Himself suffering, for He assumed with the temple of His flesh, what was inherent in that flesh, so that the passions of the flesh be mortified in us too.

We will thus hasten to resemble Christ who for our sake acquired for Himself what is ours.[112]

---

[112] Cyril of Alexandria, *Thesaurus de sancta consubstantiali trinitate* (PG 75:24).

-56-

Exalted, Anointed, and Sanctified

David sings somewhere saying: "Your throne O God is for ever and ever". He then says : "Therefore God, Your God, has anointed You with the oil of gladness more than Your companions."[113] Before this anointment, the Word reigned with the Father; how then is He to be anointed King and sanctified, being the King and the Holiest from eternity?

Though being such eternally, it is said of Him that He will possess sovereignty at the end of times. In the same way, although He is the Highest, it was said that He was exalted[114] due to the economy of the incarnation. He is exalted, and anointed[115]

---

[113] Ps. 45: 7
[114] Phil. 2: 9
[115] Ps. 45: 7

and sanctified[116] for our sakes, so that through Him the grace may also overflow in all, actually having been given to our nature [in Him], and consequently saved for the whole race. In that sense our Savior in the Gospel of John said: "And for their sakes I sanctify Myself, that they also may be sanctified in truth."[117] All that is in Christ has been given to us. He did not receive this sanctification for Himself, being Himself the Sanctifier, but received it to deliver it to our nature through Himself, becoming thus the way and the beginning of the blessings happening to us. In that sense He said "I am the way"[118] i.e., through whom Divine grace descends on us to exalt, sanctify, glorify and deify our nature in Christ first![119]

---

[116] John 17: 19
[117] John 17: 19
[118] John 14: 6
[119] Cyril of Alexandria, *Thesaurus de sancta consubstantiali trinitate* (PG 75:20).

-57-

Grace for Grace

About these sayings: "All authority has been given to Me"[120] and "Glorify Your Son"[121] [..] when the Son asks something of His Father, or is said to have received something from Him, He does not do this as Word as if He lacked glory or any other thing, but does it according to the economy (of salvation). For He receives whatever He receives humanly due to His having taken the form resembling us.[122] But as God he is perfect.

As for man, alone and on his own, even if he receives any blessings, yet he rapidly loses them, which is exactly what happened to Adam, so that due to sin he was found naked of the grace previously

---

[120] Matt 28: 18
[121] John 17: 1
[122] cf. Philo 2:6 ff

given him. In order that we should not fall again into the same situation, it was necessary that the unchangeable Word of God become man, and should ask from the Father the gifts that come from Him to be stored securely through Him in our nature, for He who receives them is unchangeable and constant.

Since grace had this new beginning, it remains permanently in Christ, and He transmits to us the same, because we are all in Him due to His having become man and having put on the same flesh that is ours.[123]

---

[123] Cyril of Alexandria, *Thesaurus de sancta consubstantiali trinitate* (PG 75:23).

-58-

Transfiguration

From the following fact we can prove that, many as were the actions that He repeatedly promised us that He would perform in due season, He even in part anticipated the appointed time in the performance of them, for our edification, that we might be fully convinced that whatsoever He has spoken will assuredly come to pass: He said that full of glory would be the resurrection of the Saints, for "then, He says, shall the righteous shine forth as the sun in the Kingdom of their Father."[124] In order that He might be believed to speak truth, He granted the sight thereof before the time to the disciples, for He "took Peter and James and John, and went up into the mountain, and was transfigured before them"[125] and "His

---

[124] Matt. 13:43
[125] Luke 9:28

Face did shine as lightning, and His garments became white as snow."[126]

---

[126] Matt. 17:2. See also On John 20:22; See *The Catechetical Lectures of St Cyril of Alexandria,* LFC 2 (London: Oxford Press 1845), 676.

-59-

Breath of Life

And how did the Son restore (humankind)? by slaying death through the death of his Holy Flesh, and raising up the human race to a mounting incorruption. For Christ was raised for our sake. Therefore in order that we might learn that it is this one who was the creator of our nature in the beginning, and who sealed us by the Holy Spirit, the Savior again for us bestows the Spirit though a visible inbreathing on the Holy disciples, as on the firstfruits of our renewed nature. For Moses writes concerning our creation of Old, that he breathed into his face of the breath of life.[127] As therefore from the beginning he was fashioned and came to be, so too is he renewed. And just as then he was formed in the image of His creator, so too now,

---

[127] Gen. 2:7

through participation in the Spirit, he is refashioned to the likeness of his maker.[128]

---

[128] In John 20:22-33 Jn 20:22-33 in Cyril of Alexandria, *Commentary on the Gospel of John*, LFC 48 (London: Oxford Press, 1885), 135.

-60-

The Ascension

It was necessary, then to lead human nature up to the summit of all good, and not only to set it free from death and sin, but to raise it already even to the heavens themselves, and to display man a sharer and fellow worshipper with angels. And just as by his own resurrection he opened a new way for us to be able to escape from corruption, so it was necessary to open for us the passage heavenwards too, and to send in the presence of the Father the one who had been expelled from his countenance because of Adam's transgression.

He places us in the presence of the Father, having departed into heaven as the firstfruits of humanity. For just as, being himself Life by nature, he is said to have died and risen again for our sake, so too, ever beholding his own Father, and in turn also being seen by his own Father, he is said to be manifested now (that is , when he became man, not for his own sake but for us) as man. And therefore this one thing was seen to be lacking in his dispensation towards us, our ascension into heaven itself, as in Christ, the firstfruits and he first of All.[129]

---

[129] John 16:7 in Cyril of Alexandria, *Commentary on the Gospel of John*, LFC 48 (London: Oxford Press, 1885), 618-19.

-61-

To Life

For since the life-giving Word of God was living in the flesh. He transformed it to his own proper good that is to life, and according to the manner of the inexpressible union, suitably rendered it wholly life-giving, as he is himself by nature. For this reason the boy of Christ gives life to those who partake of it. For it expels death, whenever it comes to be in those who are dying, and expels corruption, bearing in itself perfectly the Word who abolishes corruption.[130]

---

[130] Cyril of Alexandria, *Commentary on the Gospel of John*, LFC 48 (London: Oxford Press, 1885), 520.

-62-

To Overcome

For Christ overcame it for us as man, being also in this a beginning and gate and way for human nature. For we who were fallen and vanquished of old have conquered and have overcome on account of the one who overcame as one of us and for our sake. For if he conquered as God, it profits us nothing, but if as man, we have overcome in Him.[131]

---

[131] John 20:22-33 in Cyril of Alexandria, *Commentary on the Gospel of John*, LFC 48 (London: Oxford Press, 1885), 657.

-63-

To Live

If then, He (Christ) should say these things as man, you will receive it in this way: Christ is for us a pattern and beginning and image of the divine way of life, and He displayed clearly how and in what manner it is fitting for us to live.[132]

---

[132] John 17:6-8 in Cyril of Alexandria, *Commentary on the Gospel of John*, LFC 48 (London: Oxford Press, 1885), 316.

-64-

Trampled Death by Death

We confess that the very Son Begotten of God the Father, the Only- Begotten God, impassable though he is in his own nature, has (as the Bible says) suffered in flesh, for our sake and the he was in the crucified body claiming the sufferings of his flesh as his own impassibly. By nature life and personally the Resurrection ... "by God's Grace" he tested death for every man[133] surrendering his body to it.[134] With unspeakable power He trampled on death to become in His Own flesh first the "first-born of the dead"[135] and "first fruits of those asleep"[136] in order that he might

---

[133] Heb. 2:9
[134] cf. John 11:25
[135] Col. 1:18
[136] 1 Cor. 15:20

blaze the trail for human nature's return to incorruptibility.[137]

---

[137] Cyril of Alexandria, *Select Letters,* Oxford Early Christian Texts, ed. and trans. L.L Wickham, (Oxford: Claredon Press, 1983), 21-23.

-65-

To Bless

For the very reason that the Holy Virgin gave fleshly birth to God substantially united with flesh we declare her to be Mother of God, not because the Word's Nature somehow derived it is origin from flesh [...] He had no need of temporal birth for his own nature. No, he meant to bless the very origin of our existence, through a woman's giving birth to his united with flesh. He meant too that the curse on the whole race, which dispatches our earthly bodies to death, should cease as well as the words (from now on rendered null and void by Him) "in sorrow you shall bear children"[138] and He intended to prove true the prophet's utterance "death waxed strong and swallowed and again God took away every tear from every

---

[138] Gen. 3:16

countenance."[139] This is our reason for affirming of him that the personally blessed marriage by his Incarnation as well as by responding to the invitation to leave for Cana in Galilee along with the holy apostles.[140]

---

[139] Isa. 25:8
[140] Cyril of Alexandria, *Select Letters* Oxford Early Christian Texts, ed. and trans. L.L.Wickham, (Oxford: Claredon Press, 1983), 27-29.

-66-

To Make Holy

Seasonably comes He at length to the beginning of miracles, even if he seems to have been called to it without set purpose. For a marriage feast being held (it is clear that it was altogether holy), the mother of the Savior is present, and Himself also being bidden come together with His own disciples, to work miracles rather than to feast with them, and yet more, to sanctify the very beginning of the birth of man: I mean so far as appertains to the flesh. For it was fitting that He, Who was renewing the very nature of man, and refashioning it all for the better, should not only impart His blessings to those already called into being, but also prepare before grace for those soon to be born, and make holy their entrance into being.[141]

---

[141] John 2 in Cyril of Alexandria, *Commentary on the Gospel of John,* LFC 43 (London: Oxford Press, 1874), 200f.

-67-

Seed of Immortality

Even through death, which by transgression sprang on us, compels the human body to the debt of decay [...] yet since Christ is in us through his flesh, we shall surely rise. For as if one took a spark and buried it amid much stubble, in order that the seed of fire preserved might lay hold of it, so in us too our Lord Jesus Christ hid life though his own flesh and inserts it as a seed of immortality, abolishing the whole corruption that is in us.[142]

---

[142] John 6:54 in Cyril of Alexandria, *Commentary on the Gospel of John*, LFC 43 (London: Oxford Press, 1874), 533.

-68-

To Restore

It was not otherwise possible for man, being of a nature which perishes, to escape death, unless he recovered that ancient grace, and partook once more of God who holds all things together in being and preserves them in life through the son in the Spirit. Therefore His Only-Begotten Word has become a partaker of flesh and blood,[143] that is, he has become man—though being Life by nature, and begotten of the Life that is by Nature, that is, of God the Father—so that, having united himself with the flesh which perishes according to the law of its own nature, [...] He might restore it to his own life and render it through Himself a partaker of God the Father [...] and wears our nature, refashioning it to His own life. And He Himself is also in us, for we have all

---

[143] Heb .2:14

become partakers of Him, and have Him in ourselves through the Spirit, for this reason we have become "partakers of the divine nature"[144] and are reckoned as sons.[145]

---

[144] 2 Pet. 1:4
[145] John 14:20 in Cyril of Alexandria, *Commentary on the Gospel of John*, LFC 48 (London: Oxford Press, 1881), 485-6.

www.ingramcontent.com/pod-product-compliance
Lightning Source LLC
Chambersburg PA
CBHW020909090426
42736CB00008B/545